II

MW01047716

a short book on a long walk

J. Larry Vaughan II

CONTENTS

ACKNOWLEDGMENTS

I don't think I have had an original thought in my life. I have had a couple of interesting ideas, but nothing I would call original. My decision to write this book was based on a couple of thoughts. First, I'm getting tired of repeating myself. Second, I wanted to get my thoughts down before the gears started slipping. I've been misplacing items lately. It's probably nothing, however I wanted to write a few things down before I started hiding my own easter eggs.

I feel like I should probably warn you about my writing style. You should be able to tell fairly quickly that I'm not a trained writer. I'm a trained therapist and a trained musician and a trained husband. Not a trained writer (for example, I use too many parenthetical statements). I hope it's not off putting. Regarding my brevity, this book (pamphlet) is for a very specific target audience. I have a lot to say on the subject, but you probably don't want me to ramble on (besides, you may currently have the attention span of a ferret on crystal meth). So I'll get to the point.

I have been fortunate to have very two special groups of people in my life. Teachers who have shaped me and challenged me and taught me about the intricacies of human behavior. And my Clients who have been living textbooks, teaching me by allowing me into their lives in the most transparent way.

Among those clients have been some that have done real battle. Gladiator type stuff. Some have lost and some have won. But all have fought with a tenacious spirit, and it's these soldiers who were on my mind as I wrote this book. I wish you were all still here.

1

INTRODUCTION

George Gould's work, "Anomalies and curiosities in medicine" (1900) talks about a young man named Edward Mordrake. He was born into wealth and prosperity, and was himself a fine physical specimen. He was also a scholar and fine musician. Life was pretty good, except for one thing. He had an additional face on the back of his head. Complete with eyes and mouth. The eyes of Edward's extra face would follow objects in the room, and the face could smile and sneer, showing various emotions. The "devil twin" (Edward's term) never spoke out loud, but Edward claimed he could hear it talk, and it wasn't very nice either. Edward claims to have been kept up at night by the twin, who whispered to him repeatedly things only spoken of in hell. Edward took his own life when he was 23 years old, asking that the devil twin be destroyed before he was buried, to insure that his torment did not extend into the afterlife.

There are some doubts about the historical accuracy of the story, still the similarities between Mordrake and my clients who have suffered from chemical issues are striking. I have had countless Mordrakes sit with me in my office. Fine human specimens, having everything one could wish for. But they also had a devil twin. A chemical relationship that began (as most relationships do) with great hope and promise. Only to find themselves in a conjoined partnership that even the most skilled surgeons would find hopeless.

Mordrake (if he was real) took his life because the pain he was experiencing exceeded his ability to cope with that pain. And because he didn't see any relief in the future.

Maybe you know how he felt? Trapped? Stuck? Miserable? I heard an Old Timer describe it as Buzzard's Luck: Can't kill nothin' and nothin' will die. Well, I'm glad you're here. Buzzard's luck and all.

By the way, maybe we should introduce ourselves. I am a therapist. I have some letters after my name that I'm sure you don't care about. I've been working with people for quite a few years. How long? Well, I'm old enough to know better and still young enough to get into some trouble. I'm not sure my degrees or my experience matter much to you anyway. You probably want to know one thing: Can I help you? The answer to that is this: I don't know. I do know I'm willing to try (that's why I wrote this book). I'll bet you're willing to try too, since you're reading this (unless you're my mother, who will tell me how great it is and that Oprah needs to add it to her book club).

I'd like to know a few things about you before we get started. You can write your answers in the book or just think about the questions, it's up to you.

Name:

Age:

Why are you reading this book?

What chemicals do you like to use?

What did you used to care about that you no longer do?

What do you think about your future?

Tell me about the people who are worried about you.

Do you think you are ready to start making some small changes?

Here comes the most important thing I will say in this book: There is a way out of where you are and it can get better. I've never been accused of being an optimist, but I'm certain of this fact: There is a way out and it can get better. I've been to celebrations and funerals, and I have come away convinced. There is a way out and it can get better. **Pain has a way of distorting our perception of time and our field of vision.** I'll give you an example. Have you ever had food poisoning? That's a pretty long night, right? 8 hours seems like 80. It doesn't seem like the night will ever end. But you found out it does. **Every night ends, no matter how long or how hard it is.**

I remember a particularly tough night I had last year. I'm hearing Red from Shawshank Redemption play in my head, "...that was the longest night of my life..." Pain distorts out perception. Because of that I think the **best thing we can do when we are in pain is to listen to someone who is not.** You might find some objective truth in there somewhere. Here's my objective truth for you right now (stolen from the same movie): Hope is a good thing, maybe the best of things.

This short book is written for those of you who are miserable. You are in pain. You are misunderstood. And for a while you found out that using chemicals made that pain go away. It worked like magic (because it is). But when the magic faded you found a kind of double pain. You had the pain that preceded the chemical use, and then the chemical use added a pain of its own. So it looked kind of like this: You were not comfortable in your own skin, then you were, now its worse than is was before. Basically, you're stuck.

Well, maybe you will just grow out of it.

Here's something we don't talk a lot about in addiction circles. In my community there's basically two camps of people. One group teaches that you need AA or NA and that medicine and addiction professionals are either dangerous or secondary.

Another group teaches that AA and NA (and all the other A's) are nothing more than a cult. They preach that you need prescribed chemicals and educated professionals to help you overcome your chemical problem. The truth is there's a third reality. Maybe you don't need either. Maybe you will just grow out of it. I've seen it happen before. If you have tried to fix this on your own (and failed) maybe you should read this book. But if chemical use has become a problem it makes sense to try to fix it on your own first. Why involve a bunch of people to correct a problem if you can fix it yourself?

My dad was a very helpful father, and he was interested in me developing into a fully functioning adult. Whenever I asked for his help he would usually ask if I had tried to fix it myself. His help was usually dependent on the answer. I remember him asking me to clean the fish tank when I was a little guy. I knew the rule about Try First, then ask for help. I remember being perplexed about how a fish tank could even get dirty in the first place. The fish are taking a constant bath. But Dad was a reasonable man who usually (always) knew what he was talking about. The only tools I had ever used to clean anything at that point in my life were a vacuum cleaner and a broom. I didn't think the broom would do anything at all. So I used a vacuum cleaner. In the full fish tank. After we bought a new vacuum cleaner, Dad taught me how to properly clean a fish tank.

So if you haven't tried to fix your problem on your own, give it a shot. Hopefully you'll do better than I did on the fish tank. Help will be here if you need it.

I'm reminded of a client who definitely had a chemical abuse problem. By any assessment this guy needed some help with his problem. But his problem wasn't chemical, it was relational. As in, he was trying to be in a relationship with a self absorbed, mean, and dishonest wife. When the relationship ended (thankfully) the chemical issue did as well. I remember asking him about his drinking a few months after the divorce was final. His answer: "I don't need to drink anymore." For those of you who might think he was using the relationship as an excuse to drink, I would point out that you never met his wife. I did meet her, and after talking to her for 5 minutes I wanted to drink. Hard.

The point is, maybe you don't need a therapist or AA or this book or medication or any other tool. Do it yourself and save yourself a lot of time and money. But do me a favor: If you handle this on your own don't go bragging about it to everyone. The truth is that your ability to manage this problem on your own has less to do with your will power and a lot more to do with the size of your problem.

Maybe you have tried to manage your issue on your own with minimal success. Then you might want to keep on reading.

I'm not going to talk much about specific chemicals in this book. You know what you like. And they are really all the same to me. I don't see much difference in heroin and chardonnay. I know successful users of alcohol and marijuana, and I know people whose lives have been wrecked by grocery store supplements. So when you are reading this book, whenever you see the word, "chemicals" just insert your drug of choice. I should also add a quick word about gambling, sex, shopping, eating and internet (and other) addictions. I consider these to be chemical problems as well. The chemical we are dealing with in behavioral addictions just happens to be neurological. Behavioral addicts are just robbing the pharmacy that is between their ears. So this book can apply to you as well.

Can I ask a couple of questions?

I'm wondering something right now. How long did it take for the pain to arrive? Was it quick and sudden? Was is a long slow trajectory? Can you remember when it started? Here's a headline I read recently: "Drunk Florida Man Tried to Use Taco as ID After Accidentally Setting His Car on Fire." Sometimes we call this a wake up call. Other times we call it Tuesday. We can guess that this guy didn't just start using chemicals this week. Sounds like a pro to me.

Most people who develop a problem with chemicals have early success. The darkness creeps in like a stalking cat. Next thing you know there is a set of powerful jaws around your head.

I would like to help you pry those jaws away. I would like to help you find some peace and rest. I think I can help. I have seen it before. And while I know you are unique, there are some common features about the pain you are experiencing that you and I can focus on.

Let me start by telling you that this is going to be hard. Probably harder than anything you have done in your whole life. Even the most successful among us experience hours, days, and even weeks when the most attractive idea is just to give up. I know you just want to feel good again. To get there you are going to have to lower your expectations a little bit. Really your first goal might be to not feel terrible. This may take a while. Then you might consider a new goal: Don't feel awful (that's just a hair better than terrible). Every person is unique, so you may skip some stages or you may add some of your own. But it is going to take some time before you feel better. Longer than 28 days. Longer than 90 days. Less than 365. Somebody needs to tell you: This is not going to be fun. I've heard some people in recovery say this: "Now that I'm chemical free I'm high on life. And that high is better than any chemical high I ever had." Horseshit. The only way that is true is if they didn't know what they were doing with their chemicals. Maybe their life is better. I'll buy that. Maybe they're more productive. Sure. BUT A BETTER HIGH? I don't think so. I've had extreme natural highs in life. The birth of my daughters, a majestic beach wedding, summiting a mountain, kayaking a class V river in Colorado, and spiritual ecstasy to name just a few. I could top all of that with 5 minutes and eighty bucks. The neurochemical response when aided by outside chemicals is just superior. Any change you make is going to be difficult and it's going to take time. And there won't be tons of fun to be had in the process.

I remember a client who had a fondness for a certain plant that came from the earth. He came to me under the strong encouragement (ok, threats) of his wife. He did the work, but it was hard. I remember meeting with both he and his wife a few months after things started to improve. She grinned and said to him, "You probably ought to tell Larry what his contact name is in your phone." He looked a little embarrassed and said, "Dr. Funkiller." That was a pretty great day. Not because I like to kill fun (I really don't), but because we were on the other side of the worst of it. I still get an annual Christmas text from him using that moniker.

Probably the hardest part of the work ahead is this: I'm going to ask you for some specific behaviors for which you will not receive an immediate reward. It feels (and is) like you are being asked to work at a hard job without know what your salary will be. In fact, imagine being told that a salary will come sometime in the future and you're not told when. No one would take a job like that. Here's an added complication: Your current "job" with chemical use gives you a daily paycheck. The time between the behavior (chemical use) and the reward (the high) is a matter of minutes. To try a life without chemicals is like going from a microwave to a crock pot. Actually it's worse than that. Imagine you eat an egg every morning for breakfast. You get this egg from a fast food restaurant. I'm asking you to consider not going to the restaurant. I want you to buy a chicken. Build a pen for it. Raise it in your yard. Feed it. And wait. There's a good egg coming, but it's going to be a while. You are going to like this egg better when it shows up, but you are going to hate me for making the suggestion, especially when a pretty good egg is just down the street.

Before we get started

You have some big decisions facing you right now. I don't want you to rush this process. Whether you decide to cut back or quit or keep the same level of use, I want you to slow down the decision process. Everything is going to be slow about this process if you do it right. Weigh your options, consider the alternatives. Before you decide to make a life changing decision take a month and think about it. I know you're probably experiencing pressure to change and to change fast, but my experience is that if you bow to that external pressure the change will be short lived. Do me a favor: Tell everyone around you to Back Off! Give yourself some space and time to think. Let's just agree, based on the fact that you are reading this book and not 50 Shades of Grey, that some level of change is in order. But how much change and what to change and when to change requires careful thought and consideration.

2

LET'S GET STARTED

I want to talk to you about a few things. First I want
to talk about the brain, that 3 pound organ between
your ears. I also want to make a distinction between
the brain and it's 80 billion neurons and your mind.
When I talk about your mind I'm talking about your
memories and emotions and your plans and
relationships. Basically, your conscious will. I know
that stuff is housed in your brain, but most people
seem to understand the divergence. There is a
difference between what your brain is craving and
what your mind reasons is best for you. That's the
difference. I also want to talk about your body and
your community. Ready? Here we go.

3

THE BRAIN

Is it OK with you if I keep this part really simple? I'm
not a neurologist, and you're probably not one either
(a neurologist would definitely not buy a short book
about addiction), so let's not complicate this any more
than we have to.

Your brain likes a certain chemical. Actually your
brain loves a certain chemical. There's a megaphone
in your brain called the Anterior Cingulate (AC).
That's where the Wants and Needs live. Cravings are
born there. Reason and Logic don't go into that
room. Reason and Logic are why you bought this
book. Reason and Logic are why you are considering
divorcing the chemical your brain loves. The Anterior
Cingulate region is aware of pain, but its answer to
the pain is simple and primal: More Chemicals. So
there is a kind of war going on in your brain right

now. The rooms in your head all agree that life is hard right now. The Frontal Cortex (home base for Reason and Logic) suggests avoiding chemicals. The Anterior Cingulate suggests more chemicals. This is miserable, right?

Here's some more bad news: There is a clear pathway of communication between these two regions of the brain, but increased chemical use erodes these pathways. Meaning, the AC and the Frontal Cortex (FC) can usually have a healthy debate, but repeated chemical use diminishes the ability of the FC to be heard. The takeaway: Anterior Cingulate wins the fight. The bottom line for you: If you want to live a chemical free life (or manage your chemical use better) then you have to get your Frontal Cortex in the gym. You have to strengthen that region of your brain in order to compete with the steroid strength of the Anterior Cingulate.

This next part is going to anger some people in my field. Which is fine with me, since this book is not for them. They are not in pain. You are. And this is just for you. Here it is: There are dozens of ways you can strengthen your Frontal Cortex. Not just one way. There is no magic bullet. Our industry is full of evangelists who claim to have found the way out for you. Some suggest meetings (AA and NA), some suggest medication. Others suggest spiritual exercises. You can read countless books on the Cure for addiction.

It doesn't matter how your strengthen your Frontal Cortex. What matters is THAT you do it. And you're going to have to do it with little to no motivation to do so. If you are in pain from the chemicals then your motivation for most things is going to be zapped. I had a client say to me the other day, "Why do I have to give myself a pep talk to just get in the shower?" You get that, right? People who are not in pain think that's crazy. You understand.

It's like obesity. Why do we have an obesity problem in the most advanced country in the world? Everybody knows what is good for you (banana) and what is not (oreos). The Frontal Cortex suggests banana, but the Anterior Cingulate shouts for the oreos. I woke up this morning, Monday morning, and went downstairs to see a rainy dreary day outside. I looked on the counter and there was a banana and some oreos. It's Monday and it's raining. I picked the oreos. Why? When things aren't going my way, when life is less than I had hoped for at that given moment, I tend to listen to my Anterior Cingulate. And my Anterior Cingulate has never asked for a banana (or, for that matter, anything else that is "good" for me).

So you need to strengthen the Frontal Cortex. To do this you need to engage in an activity that is unfamiliar to you. You can go to 12 step meetings.

You can go back to school. Join a gym or a book club. Pick up a new hobby. Learn a foreign language. Take a second job. Volunteer in your community. When you are doing something that is unfamiliar that requires cognitive attention you are strengthening your Frontal Cortex. You don't want to do this. You don't have the motivation to do this. Do it anyway. You are already in pain, how much worse could it be?

I'll show you how this works. I'd like to teach you a percussion rudiment. You don't need drum sticks, just use your hands. It is called a Paradiddle.

Great name, right? Using your hands, use this sequence: RLRR (right, left, right, right). Now switch it, LRLL (left, right, left, left). That's a paradiddle. Now practice and see how fast you can get with that sequence (this exercise only works if you were not a drummer before you picked up this book). Put on some music and see if you can keep time with a song using the Paradiddle. Seriously, go spend 5 minutes on this. I'll wait right here until you get back.

What does this have to do with addiction? While you were learning the paradiddle and perfecting your timing and technique your Frontal Cortex was lit up like a Christmas Tree. More good news: Your Anterior Cingulate was mostly dormant. Let's say it took you 5 minutes to master that. You're 5 minutes closer to your goal. Here's the flip side: If you are a drummer, doing paradiddles for 5 minutes is automatic, and produces the opposite effect: It allows the AC to run like a wildfire.

So if you know how to weave baskets, for God's sake, don't weave baskets! If you're a good cook but a lousy mechanic, learn how to change the oil. Your brain is not that bright. Meaning, it's not particularly logical in the AC region. Your brain is always learning, and it is busy making correlations between your behavior and the response you get from that behavior. Sometimes with repetitive behavior, Over Learning comes into play. If you flip on the light switch in your room and suddenly your experience a Dopamine dump in your brain, and if this happens a few times, your brain will start craving light switches (I told it was not that bright). But the brain is malleable, in that over time, you can "overwrite" a strongly held previous truth. But even after the overwriting process is complete, you will still experience moments of faint connection to the previous truth.

Here's an example of that: Growing up in Lexington KY we used Crest toothpaste. Always. I don't know why (4 out of 5 dentists?), but that was our brand. My mom's parents lived in Eastern Kentucky, and life there was pretty chaotic at times. If you were my therapist I'd tell you ALL about it, but you're not. My grandparents used Colgate toothpaste. Always. This was 40 years ago. But even today, whenever I use

Colgate toothpaste, I'm projected right back to my grandparents house, and I feel a slight tinge of anxiety and apprehension. I always buy Crest. My wife buys Colgate. It's not a big deal either way, but after all these years my brain still reminds what my life was like 40 years ago just based on what brand of toothpaste I use.

So now you know why most people who work in addiction ask you to be careful about the places you go and the people you see in early recovery.

Let me ask you a few questions:

How old were you when your brain began regularly
associating a certain chemical with pleasure?

What activities does your brain associate with your
chemical?

What places does your brain associate with your
chemical?

Which of these places and activities will be easiest to
avoid for a while? Which will be hardest?

4

THE BODY

You have really done a number on your body, haven't you? I'm sure nutrition and exercise have been the last thing on your mind lately. Trying to recover from chemicals with a body that has been abused by chemicals is like starting behind the line of scrimmage. It would be nice if we could just go back to the factory for a quick makeover or tune up. Since we can't do that we're going to have to do this the slow way. Maybe you're picking up a theme by now? For you to get better it's going to take some time. More time than you want to take. But if we take our time and don't rush this I promise you are going to like the outcome.

I bought a couple of new chairs for one of my therapists last year. I paid about $150.00 for each one. They were made in a factory and probably took about 10 minutes to build. The chairs are broken now and I have to replace both of them. As I write this I'm looking at a rocking chair in my office. Built in 1875, this chair was built by a craftsman who took his time. You can start to see my bias coming through: Measure twice, cut once. Perfect the skill and the art remains. I would prefer you to last a good long time and enjoy a high quality of life in your remaining years, maybe even leaving a lasting legacy that trickles through the generations.

Before I go any further I want you to know a couple of things. I'm not a doctor. I didn't even stay at a Holiday Inn Express last night. I cannot prescribe medications. I can't even cure a ham. So I really want you to find a general physician and make an appointment for a full check up with blood work. Tell your doctor everything. Well, maybe not everything. If you tell your doctor what you have been thinking that might raise a few eyebrows. Tell your doctor what you have been putting in your body. Tell your doctor what has been coming out of your body. Tell your doctor how long you have been doing this. If you get a lecture at this point find another doctor. Finding the right doc can be a little tricky. Some of them have a current negative relationship with chemicals themselves. Others have not been well trained in addiction (my experience is that most physicians are under trained in the field of addiction). In my experience the docs who have overcome a chemical problem (and have been clean for at least 5 years) and the docs who have had some specific training in the area of addiction make the best candidates.

I'm going to offer some over the counter and homeopathic suggestions in a minute, but I wanted to share a quick thought about prescription medications that are designed to help those dealing with a chemical problem. Pharmaceutical companies are just coming around to the idea that there is money to be made in addiction medication. Most are still not willing to be saddled with the "addiction" label and everything that goes along with that, but minds are being turned as we speak. In 2012, Suboxone brought in a cool $1.5 billion dollars, outselling both Viagra and Adderall. The down side to Suboxone is this: It's expensive, it delays the recovery process, withdrawal symptoms are a nightmare, and good luck having a bowel movement. The upside is this: Compared to a life of active chemical use, you will be doing tons better. I've had clients stop using chemicals with and without Suboxone. My clients who do this without Suboxone are almost always in a better spot at the one year mark. My clients who are using Suboxone are better off than those still abusing chemicals at the one year mark. My takeaway from this observation (which is not based on research, just observation) is this: If you can do it without Suboxone, this is your best option. If you can't; if your only two solutions are active use or Suboxone, choose Suboxone. But I really want you to do this without Suboxone.

Your doctor may offer a variety of prescription medications to help you during your early days in recovery. If your doctor offers you a benzodiazepine, you have the wrong doc. I will talk to you about psychiatric medications in a later section, but you might not want to let your General Practitioner prescribe psychotropic drugs at all. You also don't need a prescription sleep aid. There is no pill on the market that is going to make you feel well. There is a medication that is currently in limited human trial right now called 18-MC. It looks promising but time will tell. For you, this is going to take some time. And it's going to hurt. The payoff is going to come much later than you would like, but it's coming, I promise.

Let me offer you a few suggestions that might give your body the stuff it needs during this difficult time. Talk these over with your doctor. All of these products can be found in your local health food stores or online.

In early recovery most people experience an increase in pain and anxiety. DLPA has been shown to work on both of these conditions.

Abusing chemicals, particularly in mid to late stages, produces a chaotic life. Chaos increases stress. Stress increases the production of Cortisol. Increased Cortisol production results in adrenal fatigue. The amino acid Tyrosine will be helpful in correcting this imbalance.

Regardless of the chemical you have been using, chances are good you are experiencing an electrolyte imbalance. Drinking water with lemon will be helpful for that.

You need sleep. You can't sleep. You don't need Ambien, but you do need to sleep. Your liver probably needs some repair time, and this happens mostly between 1AM and 3AM. An irregular sleep pattern will produce increased anxiety, mood swings, and poor self-control. Everything you don't need right now. L-Theanine is a supplement you might consider, along with short term use of Melatonin. Melatonin is not designed for long term use, and in increasing doses tend to produce the opposite effect it was designed for. So it may be helpful for a month or two at no more than 5mg per night. You may be thinking 5mg makes me a little sleepy, so 20mg should knock me out. You would be wrong about that.

If opiates are your thing, you're probably low in calcium, vitamin D, vitamin B-6, and iron. Find the foods rich in these vitamins and minerals and add them to your diet.

Regular cocaine use will deplete your body of Omega-3 fatty acids. Eat some fish.

If alcohol is your choice of drug, well, you're

probably low on nutrients across the board. Alcohol rids the body of more nutrients that other drugs of abuse.

Low magnesium is a common result of abusing chemicals, resulting in insomnia, anxiety, and a general feeling of weakness.

Here's what I don't want you to do (I bet you've already thought about doing it): Run to the vitamin store and start taking 18 pills a day. Quick fix, right? I want you to slow down. I'd like for you to think about restoring your body's nutrients the old fashioned way: through food. I would also like for you to consider eating 6 small meals a day (more on this later). "Never hungry, never full" would be a good goal for you.

Nobody runs a marathon on crutches. When your body is not well you are operating at a sub-optimal level. This is a hard thing you are doing right now. Set yourself up for success by getting your body in better shape. That includes exercise. Five times a week. At least 30 minutes each time. I don't care if it's dancing in the living room or doing parkour (consult your physician before beginning a work out regimen). I know you don't want to do it. I don't care what you want right now. You might want to consider not caring about what you want right now. This is the part where you are building the chicken coop so you can eventually have eggs.

Here's a few more questions for you:

How long has it been since you had a general physical (complete with bloodwork)?

Can you list the physical symptoms that are bothering you the most these days? Be as specific as possible.

On a scale from 1-10 (1 being the lowest), how would you rate your level of physical activity in the last 3 months? Whatever your number, consider raising this in increments of one over a couple of weeks, continuing that process.

5

THE MIND

I can think of about 15 mental illnesses you could be diagnosed with right now at this minute. You have gone through life with a wrecking ball (please don't sing the song) leaving carnage and chaos in your path. Now you are eliminating the one chemical (or several) that brought you the slightest bit of peace in the storm. You're a bloody mess. But you probably don't have those 15 mental illnesses. It just looks like you do. The mental anguish you are in right now is temporary.

Of course you're depressed, but it might not be an organic depression. Of course you're experiencing mood swings, but it's likely not Bipolar. You are all you think about these days, but this narcissism is temporary. You definitely have a problem with chemicals, and you likely have at least one other thing going on in your mind. It's called comorbidity. You have chemical dependence and (fill in the blank). So what is your "fill in the blank"? Here's some more bad news: We don't know. We won't know for a year or two after you stop abusing the chemicals. Yes, a year or two. We need a base line. Your chemical use has thrown off all of the readings. And it really takes that long to figure out what is going on with you. You might have a few suspects. For instance, maybe you remember experiencing clinical depression prior to abusing chemicals. When the dust settles we may find out that you still have clinical depression. But maybe not. So we are going to have to wait.

Because of this, your healthcare professional that prescribes a psychotropic medication in your first month of sobriety is doing you a disservice. You might not need Cymbalta. And if you don't need Cymbalta you sure don't want to take it, since it's no picnic to stop taking it.

I am hesitant to diagnose someone with any mental disorder other than chemical abuse or dependence within the first 18 months of sobriety. I would recommend treating the symptoms, however. If you are experiencing symptoms of anxiety I want you to treat that. Being anxious is a real threat to your sobriety. So is being depressed. But there are natural ways to treat these symptoms. Since you have recently just finished a period of your life where a chemical provided almost instant relief, it would be natural to think that medicine could do the same thing for your early sobriety. But I need to you be patient with me. I need you to be patient with yourself.

Yoga and meditation can do wonders for your anxiety (I know you just rolled your eyes at me). Once you settle into your new life without chemicals you will find that your lifestyle will be less anxious. You don't have to hide any more. You don't have to run to the pawn shop to get something out or put something in.

You will most like experience a condition known as **anhedonia**. It's the inability to experience pleasure in normally pleasurable experiences. Imagine one long case of the Blahs. Nothing sounds good. Nothing tastes good. Nothing feels good. There's a mild irritation that usually goes along with anhedonia. You are going to experience this because you have over-worked your brain with the chemical abuse. Duration of anhedonia varies, but 3-6 months is not uncommon. It can last longer or shorter than that. This is a pretty dangerous time. One thing is true about your last several months. Maybe even years. You sure did feel a lot of emotions. Some of them were great, others were terrible. But you felt. Now you don't. You miss feeling things. Anything would be better than this. So you look for things to make you feel. You know you should avoid your chemical, but maybe there's something out there that will resurrect your dead emotions.

You did hone one great quality in addiction. You

learned how to be incredibly resourceful. You learned how to get what you want. You may use this powerful skill to kick start your emotions. I'm going to ask you to not do that. If you're early in the process of sobriety and you find something that makes you feel again, you are going to turn that thing into an obsession and run it in the ground.

As soon as you start to feel better physically I want you to start working on your mind. I want you to consider where you are right now and where you have been and where you want to go. I want you to pay attention to the vast gulf between where you are right now and where you thought you were heading. How did you get here? There will be no easy answer to that question. As you start to peel back the layers you will start to uncover a complex web of early experiences and belief systems. You can't change what has happened but you can reconstruct a system of belief that will produce different results.

I wonder who taught you to embrace a chemical solution? Maybe a name came to mind. Maybe it's someone you love and admire. Maybe it's not a simple answer. I was doing some supervision with a therapist the other day. Her 17 year old client's issue was that her mom was sleeping with her boyfriend. That's messed up, right? Well, there are a lot of things that are messed up. And there's degrees of messed up. We are all messed up. Some of us hide it better than others. I don't see much difference between the scenario above and the dad who teaches his kid (by example) that having a top shelf drink at the end of the day to "relax" is how you should cope with stress. It's the same message.

This is not your fault. This is also not your parents fault. It's not society's fault. Not 100%. You are in a systemic imbalance and you have a role in it. But so does everyone in your "system". This is going to take some time, but you might want to look at everything around you and consider what and who has played a part in you arriving where you have. It's not a blame game, but if you don't assign some degree of responsibility to those who have been responsible, then that part of your system will forever remain unchanged. And change is what you need. That and a good nap.

I know this is a short book, but I also know you are already frustrated with me telling you to slow down, that the process is going to take some time. If I had quick solutions for you I would share them. I'm not even a little bit masochistic. I know some people (mainly the ones you have caused pain) would like to see you suffer a little bit. Some would like to see that to satisfy some revenge, others because they falsely think that if you are in pain it will "teach you a lesson." Well, I'm neither. You haven't hurt me and pain is a lousy long term teacher. This process takes time because it does. We are complicated creatures. Maybe you have noticed that men have nipples. Does that make any sense to you? Me either. I've had nipples for 50 years and still don't know what to do with them.

Here's another idea I'd like for you to think about. What did you like about you, early on, when you had the chemical in you? It made something better. What was it? It made something you didn't like seem smaller or less significant. What was it?

I had a client who was painfully shy and introverted. On chemicals he became somewhat of an extrovert. People seemed to like this guy. He liked that people liked this guy. So he tried to recreate the guy people liked as often as he could. I'm sure you know the end of this story. He couldn't sustain the new guy. Nobody can sustain it.

There are two words my clients use to describe early recovery: Painful and Boring. Maybe you noticed that Carnival Cruises doesn't have a ship named that. I would like to suggest you replace those words with Educational and Safe. I know that's not a ton better, but one of the great things you get to do during this time on your life is redefine your terms. The truth is you can normalize just about anything. **With consistent, willing behavior over a period of time, your mind will balance itself according to your**

behavior.

I had a job once vacuuming tennis courts (not exactly a mentally taxing venture). It was from 4am-7am every day. 4am. I didn't know there were two 4 O'clocks in the day. Waking up at 3:30am that first week was brutal (I lived across the street from the job site). I also had a job from 8am-5pm. And another one from 6pm-10pm. This was necessary, as I had made some poor choices leading up to this point in my life. You probably know what happened next. What seemed impossible in the beginning became normal after a few months. This "balancing" act is part of what kept you using chemicals as long as you did. If that principle was at work normalizing chaos, it will also work when you try to normalize a calmer life. Willing, consistent behavior over a period of time is the key here.

So maybe you have tried to correct this issue on your own with limited results. And maybe you have decided that setting limits hasn't worked so well either. Maybe you have taken your time and carefully considered all of the pros and cons and have come to the conclusion that you need to stop using chemicals.

Here's a little pearl of wisdom given to me recently by a client: **"When I don't do something to make myself feel better, I feel bad."** You might want to think about that for a minute or two. This doesn't describe all of humanity but I bet it describes you. Some people feel normal when they don't do something intentional to make themselves feel better. Here's an even stranger thought: Some people go days without thinking about how they feel. Weird, huh? In this next section I'm going to describe some behaviors I want you to do. All of them are designed to make you feel better. Eventually.

There are a few things I would like for you to focus on during your first 90 days of sobriety. I'm not really concerned whether you want to do these things or not. I would like for you to do these things in kind of a robotic way. They are just behaviors. Here they are:

1. Be in the bed resting (or sleeping) 8 hours a day.

2. Eat 3 regular meals or 6 small meals a day.

3. Sweat in exercise 4-5 times a week.

4. Talk to people who are doing life chemical free daily.

5. Don't change your relationship status.

6. Limit social media.

7. Produce something weekly.

8. Work on telling the truth every day.

9. Scale your mood daily.

10. Don't use chemicals.

I'll expand on these:

Rest for 8 hours a day (sleeping if you can).

One of the first things to go when chemicals get out of control is routine. One of the first things I want you to restore in early sobriety is routine. You will resist this (along with most of my suggestions; it's OK, I'm used to it). I want you to pick a bed time and stick to it. Pick a rising time and stick to that as well. It doesn't matter if you feel tired or sleepy. It's rest time. Doing what you feel like doing when you feel like doing it has contributed to the condition you are currently in. I frequently tell my clients in early sobriety, "I don't care how you feel." They know I care about them, but I also know their emotions are off line. Their emotions cannot be trusted at the moment and will betray them at every turn. I talk with my clients about becoming "robotic" for the short term, just going through the motions. This helps the mind, brain, and body restore the balance that is badly needed.

Eat regularly.

Three regular meals or preferably 6 small ones throughout the day. In a perfect world I would rather you not feel hunger at all. We do silly things when we get hungry. One of my girls at home (I'm not naming names, but she is the youngest) turns into King Kong when she's hungry. We call this Hangry. When we see the early signs of this we rush around to get her something to eat quickly. When we are hungry our patience is shortened along with our fuse. That's a pretty bad place to be when you are trying to avoid chemicals.

Here's another cool benefit of eating 6 small meals a day: When you put food in your mouth your brain stops whatever it is doing (craving, ruminating, scheming) and calls everyone between your ears to attention. The public address system comes over the loudspeakers and asks this one important question: "What is that?" It happens every time you put food in your mouth. It's call the Orienting Reflex. And this is valuable to you in early sobriety. Do you remember a time at a restaurant when the waiter refilled your drink and he brought you something different than you ordered? That's when the Orienting Reflex kicks in. Six small meals a day means six mini vacations from what your brain is probably obsessing about right now.

Sweat.

If I had my preference you would exercise outside. For whatever reason, treadmills and early sobriety don't mix well. I know that's not always practical, but since when did you become practical?

I know exercise isn't fun. But this is essential to your Big Comeback. When I look through my files and identify the most successful clients, all of them incorporated exercise into their routine. All of them. That's like 100%. Find an exercise routine you can tolerate and do it. Start slow and be smart about it. As in, if alcohol is your chemical, rugby is probably not your sport.

Talk to people who are doing life chemical free.

I don't care where you get your support. But this is not a solo sport. You can do it in a 12 step support group, online forum, or create your own. Think of this time like an internship. You are learning to be chemical free. Interns learn best from those who have been doing it longer than them. I would also like for you to limit your time with people who are using chemicals. I know what I am asking of you, and I know how tough this request is. I know you are tangled up with people who use chemicals, and I know you have deep emotional ties with them. I know you care about them and I know they care about you.

I'm not going to give you some bullshit song about them not being your "real" friends. I don't even know them, how could I make that judgement? But the reality is that you can't go on a diet when your friends keep taking you to Baskin Robbins. Unless you are a sociopath (I really hope you're not), you are powerfully influenced by your environment. More so than you realize. If you surround yourself with people who are intentionally living chemical free you greatly increase your chances for success. I've been doing this for quite a few years, and I can't remember a client who has been successful at living chemical free that didn't change their environment to include intentionally chemical free people.

Don't change your relationship status.

If you're single this one is easy. Stay single. I think you have something to offer someone in the future, but not right now. You are currently in Emotional ICU. A relationship would be exciting and distracting. But you won't be good at it. And it will end badly. Which causes you more pain. I don't want you to be in more pain.

If you're married or in a relationship, chances are it's pretty broken. Either your significant other is a chemical user or they aren't. Either way the relationship is probably dysfunctional. I don't want you to stay in an abusive relationship. If that's the case, find a way out, and quick. If your SO is a chemical user, ask them to not use around you and to keep your home chemical free. If they can't do that, you should consider leaving. Other than these two reasons, stick around a while.

If you liked your SO when you were using chemicals, you won't like them now. You won't like anything now. If you didn't like them while you were using, you REALLY won't like them now. Don't worry, the feelings will be mutual. Here comes my broken record: I want you to wait. You will need some relationship counseling, but that's going to come later. Optimistically in 6 months. Realistically in 12 months. You don't want the pessimistic prediction.

Limit social media.

You probably think I'm a little behind the times with this suggestion, but I'd like you to hear me out on this one. 90% of the time when social media gets mentioned in my office it has a negative connotation ("You know what that skank put on facebook?!?!"). It's a huge source of conflict and drama. You don't need more conflict and drama right now. But your brain will try to stir some up. Feeling bad or angry is better than feeling nothing. If you feel bad and angry you might find a good enough reason to pick up the chemicals again. I'm sorry your brain is working against your goals here, but if you give it some time we can change that.

Produce something weekly.

I'm not going to sugar coat this one for you. When
you were using chemicals you were harming not only
yourself, but the culture around you. You made this a
worse place to live because of your actions. This isn't
news to you. You had a front row seat for it. I want
you to start reversing that trend. Nobody comes to
end of their chemical use with their self esteem in
tact. By producing something, making something,
creating something, you can start to rebuild a
healthier view of yourself. Maybe you have some
creativity in you? Make some music or art or learn a
craft. Maybe you're not creative in the least? Find
something to do that wouldn't be done if you hadn't
been on this earth. If you pick up one piece of trash
in public and throw it away, you have produced
something. Next time you are in line at a fast food
restaurant, buy the person's meal behind you. Rake a
neighbor's yard. Change someone's flat tire. Make this
a better place to live. You owe the earth that right
now. Even under the best circumstances, your
chemical use made you oblivious to the needs of
others. What is more likely is that your chemical use
caused others quite a bit of heartache and pain. Even
as I write this there is a guy in my waiting room that
has cut an impressive path of destruction over the last
3 years. He's really the nicest guy you could ever meet,

but he has left a real trail of tears. Guess what? He doesn't like himself much right now.

Work on telling the truth every day.

I have met honest people and dishonest people. I have never met someone who has developed a problem with chemicals who was honest throughout their use. To keep the chemical use active I'm pretty sure you have had to practice some deception. In my business we dress it up a little bit and call it minimizing. For some people (and maybe for you) deception became such a regular part of their life that to lie was the default position. It became habit. Here's the irony: In order to get better you have to start telling the truth again. When you're using chemicals, an extra step is added to the communication process. Here's the equation without chemicals: A person asks you a question, you process the question, you give an answer. Your answer is honest and the degree of information given directly reflects your relationship with that person. Here's an example:

Barista: "How are you today?" Me: "I'm OK."

Banks (a mentor of mine): "How are you today?" Me: "Well, I've been having some difficulties with... blah, blah, blah."

Both honest answers, but the degree of information is measured by the depth of the relationship. Now here's the added step when chemicals have been an active part of your lifestyle:

Spouse: "What took you so long at the store?"

You run each question through a filter and try to decide which answer would have the best outcome for you. Which answer will keep your chemical use a secret and create the least amount of conflict. Now you have options to consider. Do you say:

A. I had a flat tire (she might want to see the receipt).

B. I stopped at the library to read about how to be a better husband (she might ask questions about the book).

C. Why are you always suspicious? (putting it back on her might work, but it might cause conflict too).

D. I just took a little drive to clear my head (this might actually work).

Here's what you absolutely do not say: "I thought I had an extra hour to kill so I stopped by the bar and slammed four or five shots just to get my head right. I just intended to have a couple drinks, but I started to get a little buzz and the waitress was flirting with me and I really didn't want to come home to your nagging inquisition."

I'm not going to ask you to start telling the whole truth to everyone you meet. But I do want you to work on increasing the truthfulness of your answers to the important people in your life. I don't expect that is going to be particularly easy or fun, but it will help you get through this uphill journey you are on.

Scale your mood daily.

Finally I have something easy for you to do. Buy a notebook (or set up a spreadsheet on your computer). At the end of each day I want you to assign a number to that day from 1-10. 1 if you had a horrible day. 10 if your day was amazing. 3 for meh. Think about this number for about 5 minutes and write it down. Now you're done. Do it again the next day. And every day. For the next several months. There's a couple reasons I want you to do this simple exercise. First, change comes painfully slow in this process, and this is a way to monitor your progress, kind of like a time lapse camera. After you have done this for several weeks you will be able to look back and track your progress. This is about inches, not miles. Second, you may be able to spot trouble areas by doing this. If after a few weeks you notice that Sundays are typically rated as two or three, but the rest of the week is in the five or six range, we now have a great question to ask: What's the deal with Sundays? Also, if you look back over time and see that your numbers are gradually getting lower, it might be an indication that you are missing something in your program. Don't plan of figuring this out on your own.

Don't use chemicals.

I'm not trying to Nancy Reagan you right now. I just want you to do whatever it takes to avoid the chemicals that got you in this place to start with. Using chemicals, even once, has a devastating neurochemical result. This is hard right now, the hardest thing you have ever done in your life. This is going to get easier, but that doesn't help much right now. Here's a little sliver of hope for you: The ones I know that have made it through, they are glad they pressed on. The ones that go back to the chemicals regret it. No exceptions. I'm usually not a black and white guy. I've got a ton of grey in me these days. I have never seen an exception in all my years for this rule. The odds are overwhelmingly in your favor. If you continue to work on yourself in an intentional way and avoid using chemicals to improve the quality of your life, you will come out of this far better than you were, much better than you are right now.

A few more questions to think about:

I suggested some specific behaviors in this section. Which behaviors seem out of reach for you at the moment?

What would have to change in your life in order for those goals to be met?

Thinking about where you are today, how much impact have others had on your current position? Would you take some time with this one? Maybe a day or two? The goal isn't to assign blame but to try to get a clear picture of who and what played a part in you getting here.

6

THE VILLAGE

Assuming you have tried to manage this on your own with little success, it's time for you to build a team. You have some people around you right now that are not helping matters. You may need some distance from a few of them. Let's say your problem chemical is alcohol. You regularly meet a few of your friends for happy hour. There may be nothing wrong with your friends and there is nothing wrong with happy hour. But the combination of those friends, happy hour, and you have produced miserable results. What I'm telling you is this: You are simply not strong enough right now to hang out at happy hour with your friends while they use a chemical you're trying to avoid. This principle works in a variety of areas. People on a diet don't hang out at the bakery. People on diets hang out at the gym and the juice bar. A bakery is way more fun than the gym, but we're not shooting for "fun" yet.

This is the thing I like best about the support groups that already exist in your community. When you attend an AA or NA meeting, you are surrounded by at least a few people that are trying to do what you are trying to do. This gives you strength and support. Plus, they kind of get you. People that have not developed a love affair with chemicals will think your thought process is a little strange. Imagine one month after getting out of jail for a DUI where you totaled your car and lost your job as a result. You're thinking about drinking again. If you tell that to someone who hasn't had a chemical issue they will look at you like you're an alien. It's good to be around people that understand you.

Setting yourself up for success means you will surround yourself with two groups of people. First, those who have successfully conquered chemical abuse in their lives. By "successful" I mean people who have been consequence free from chemical use for more than a year. The second group is made up of professionals who have been trained in chemical abuse. Maybe a psychologist, therapist, or life coach. You want them to at least have a Master's Degree and be licensed in your state to practice. I don't know how many sessions you need with this professional, but I know you'll likely need a few to get things ironed out.

7

HOW TO PICK A THERAPIST

Thankfully the idea of seeking help from a therapist isn't as taboo as it was a generation ago. The demand for therapy services is higher than it has ever been. There is an upside and a downside to this. Therapy services are just like any other service in your area; there are good therapists, bad therapists, and dangerous therapists. Here are a few tips to help you find the good ones:

*The internet is a good place to start. However, don't make your final decision based on Google. Read their profiles and reviews. Don't be put off by a couple of bad reviews, look at the composite of online comments. Do they take insurance? Whether or not you are going to use your insurance, you want them to be on the insurance panels. You want your therapist to be licensed in your state. If they are not licensed it's because they don't meet the basic requirements.

*Ask around. This is the best way to find a good therapist. Ask your friends if they know a good therapist. Ask them if they know any bad ones. Make a list from your internet search and from your friend's suggestions.

*Make an appointment. If your therapist has an opening the next day they might not be the best choice. Good therapists are in high demand.

*After your first session: Did you like them? Did they listen to you? Did you feel heard? Did you set some goals? Did they try to sell you the book they wrote? Who did most of the talking (you should)? Did they fall asleep (this happens)? Did they pick their nose (this also happens)?

*The duration and frequency of therapy should be up to you, within reason of course. Your therapist will likely have some input on the topic, but you might want to be cautious of a therapist who insists on a specific duration or frequency.

A cautionary word about therapy

I am a therapist. I have just recommended therapy to you. But I want you to be careful about this. Therapy can be dangerous. I wish this were not true, but it is. Good therapy can be a life saver. Bad therapy can be devastating. Unfortunately for the consumer, sometimes it's hard to tell the difference in the beginning. Please do your homework on this, and trust your intuition in the process. Don't assume because they have some parchment on their walls that they know what they are doing. I have had to do a fair amount of work repairing trauma created in a prior therapeutic relationship. I'd love to tell you some stories, but proper decorum won't allow it.

Here's one anyway: I was supervising an associate who brought me voicemails left on a client's phone by her therapist. Long, rambling, drunken, incoherent, multiple messages telling the client they need to come back to therapy. Telling the client their mental health is at stake if they don't come back to therapy. The therapist told the client the devil was trying to keep her sick and that God wanted her to get better by scheduling more sessions with him. We reported the therapist, but the licensing board did not find enough evidence to revoke his license. He's still practicing therapy in our area.

You would think the laws of supply and demand would work well here. Bad therapists who provide bad therapy would eventually end up playing guitar for a Safe Auto insurance commercial. But that's not always the case. I'm sorry there are nut balls out there operating under the guise of helping others, but that's just the reality right now. Don't avoid therapy because of this, just be careful. And if your therapist ever tells you what God wants you to do, or talks incessantly

about sports, music, or themselves, run out of there
like you stole something.

8

DO YOU NEED REHAB?

I get asked about rehab a lot. Do I need it? Where should I go? How much does it cost? Here's a few simple thoughts on the subject. First, if you're dependent on alcohol or benzodiazepines, you do need medical detox. Stopping these substances abruptly can kill you. Once you have detoxed you can ask yourself the rehab questions. Have you tried to quit on your own? Have you seen a therapist? Have you gone to an outpatient clinic? If you answered "yes" to these questions and your still struggling with chemicals, it's time for rehab. Pick a 30 day inpatient facility based on your income level. Want a nice one? Go to Pavilion in Asheville, NC. Are you broke? Go to Salvation Army in Dayton, OH. Somewhere in between? Try Cumberland Heights in Nashville, TN. As with therapists, there are good, bad, and dangerous rehabs. I got a call this week from one of the dangerous ones. They wanted to treat me to a day of food and entertainment to talk about their amazing program. I told him I wasn't a fan of his program and gave him my reasons why. But the rehab is still full.

If you haven't tried localized support (outpatient, therapist, support groups) try that first.

If you get out of rehab and you continue to use, go back. If you get back from your second rodeo and you continue to use, go back again. But go to a longer one this time. I don't know what it will take for you to learn to live successfully without chemicals. That's your job. You know yourself better than anyone else.

9

ANECDOTAL OBSERVATIONS

I want to tell you about a few things I have seen in my practice. These observations are not based on research, just observation.

I have noticed some patterns over the years. People who have been in my office with a chemical problem tend to have certain qualities and characteristics. There are exceptions, of course. But when I begin to see patterns I pay attention. I am telling you about these characteristics for a couple of reasons. First, so you can watch for these qualities in your child. The presence of these qualities do not necessitate the presence of a future chemical problem, but as parents we can be watchful and be proactive in helping our child build positive coping skills for possible future stressors. Secondly, you may find yourself identifying with some of these characteristics. If so, you can look for corresponding coping skills and find ways to order your day for optimal experience.

I have noticed one common denominator is all of these characteristics: They make life just a little more difficult. Life is kind of hard as it is, but these characteristics make it a little more so.

I have noticed a high number of clients who report having a **high reactive temperament**. Temperament is evident in infancy, and a high reactive child is usually observed as a "difficult" child. Restless, very responsive to attachment, requiring constant attention. We know through pretty good research that children with a high reactive temperament have a high level of stress hormones. These individuals may find normally soothing activities to be inadequate and wind up looking for chemical solutions for some relief. Jerome Kagan and Nathan Fox have done some excellent research on high reactivity in children, you may want to check them out.

Introverts also make up a higher percentage of clients with substance issues in my practice. I'm not entirely certain why this is true, and maybe it's only true for my practice and not the general population. I've read the research. It's not conclusive. There are too many variables to consider here. For instance, is it introversion or depression or isolation? We just can't measure that in human behavior yet.

I do know that chemicals are beneficial socially to the introvert, allowing them to feel more comfortable in social circles. I also know that our culture values extroversion over introversion (thanks to Susan Cain's book, "Quiet"), and that early chemical use may be seen as improving one's stock. Also, introverts are less likely to reach out for help in the early stages of chemical use, thus allowing the condition to progress before it gets some attention.

Above average intelligence is another quality I see in my clients frequently. I remember a media campaign years ago that said, "Drugs are for Dummies." My experience has been the opposite. Of all my anecdotal observations, this one seems to be the most consistent. In fact, when someone presents in my office with a chemical issue I begin with the assumption that they have an elevated level of intelligence and I wait to be proven wrong. Intelligent people have the capacity to see more, feel more, know more. But high intelligence does not necessarily mean they have the capacity to process more. Imagine if every day were Thanksgiving. You know that bloated 4pm feeling on that day? The body has taken on more food than it can process. I think this is true with intelligent people on a daily basis. Due to their increased intelligence they are taking in more information than they can process. Frequently, they feel the mental pressure from this intake. At this point I bet you could guess what could work very effectively at relieving that pressure. Sometimes I call this (for lack of a better term) emotional constipation.

Here's another quality I see frequently: **Cognitive (and Behavioral) Disinhibition**. OK, that's two qualities, but they are connected.

John Belushi. That's who comes to mind when I think of disinhibition. Mr. Excess. In simple terms, Cognitive disinhibition is the ability to think completely out of the box. Behavioral inhibition is the ability to follow through with that crazy idea.

One of Mr. Belushi's favorite games was Cocaine Chicken. He would cut an ounce of cocaine in one line several feet long and then challenge a friend. John would start at one end of the line, the challenger at the other. First one to the middle wins. John always won. Now here's a question: Who could think of such a game? Well, John could. But even if you thought up the game what quality would you have to possess to actually carry it out? Guts? Cajones? That's disinhibition. This quality is legendary among celebrities and musicians, but it exists with similar results among the general population. Incidentally, Mr. Belushi once told Carrie Fisher he was worried about her drug use. That's when you know you have a real problem. John was a creative genius. That coupled with his disinhibition is why he is no longer with us.

A theme is emerging here. Imagine these qualities in one person: An introverted individual with a high reactive temperament, possessing both disinhibition and an elevated intelligence. This is my definition of a perfect storm. We can recall the names: Michael Jackson, Philip Seymour Hoffman, Elvis, Robin Williams. Those are the ones we all know about. Who comes to your mind as you read that list of qualities? Someone you know? Maybe you?

So what if you recognize yourself in this list of traits? Well, personality is pretty well fixed, but you can move the lines a little bit. And that's precisely what I suggest you do. Actually, these are wonderful qualities and it would be tragic to eliminate them altogether. You don't need less information, just a better processor. You can't become an extrovert, but you can learn to be with people more comfortably. You will benefit from your hyper awareness, but you will need to learn how to turn it off from time to time to give yourself some space to let everything digest. Your intelligence is an asset, just find the pause button that is not chemical in nature.

I don't want you to stop being you. I know this chemical thing has your identity skewed. And I know you've been taking a beating from your friends and family. Maybe even your employer and the courts. Probably even from yourself. But even though we have never met I'm willing to bet there's a pretty cool person just beneath the scabs. And when the scabs go away you'll be left with a few scars. But you know what? Scars are really kind of beautiful. A symbol of survived pain. A symbol of victory in a battle that cost you something.

10

CLOSING TIME

A client sent me a picture the other day. A remarkable picture. He was holding a newborn baby. He is a recovered opiate addict. It's been years since he last used. He's gotten his life together since he quit. He has a good job, a nice house, a supportive family, a happy wife, and new little baby. But all of that pales in comparison to the one thing this guy found in sobriety. His eyes are clear. The baby is cute in the picture, and he's smiling like any proud papa. It's his gaze that caught me. I've seen that look in others. That look says two things: I'm not hiding anything and I like who I have become.

More than anything that's what I want for you. However you do it. I want that for you.

11

A FINAL OBITUARY

This just happened. While I was editing this book and getting it ready to send to the publisher I got a phone call.

I had known Jimmy for more than 25 years. We were pretty close in the beginning. I was working with teenagers then, and he was definitely a kid at heart. I used him as a chaperone on several trips and outings. The kids loved him and I enjoyed his company. But even back then he was doing battle with chemicals. He tried a few times to beat this beast but it was too much.

In some ways he was my own personal Robin Williams. I never knew a funnier person. There was a time when he was trying to wrangle the addiction. He was trying to discover what co morbid condition kept him uncomfortable in his own skin. This search led him to Vanderbilt University where a team of physicians was interviewing him for the possibility of ADD. One of the surgeons was making small talk during the introduction and mentioned that his father was also from Kentucky and used to breed horses there. Without missing a step Jimmy said, "How did he do that? Did he use a stump?" The guy just didn't have a filter between his mind and his mouth.

One Christmas Jimmy and I rented a couple of costumes on a whim. I was Frosty, Jimmy was Rudolph. We drove around all night visiting restaurants. We would walk through the restaurant greeting the patrons, talking to the kids. In each restaurant the manager would come up and ask what we were doing there. Our answer was the same at each one: "Brad from Corporate sent us over." Apparently, there's a Brad at every corporate branch. We got a lot of free food and a ton of laughs that night.

I was talking to a family member today. She said some well meaning relatives were speculating on whether Jimmy was now resting peacefully in heaven or being tormented in hell. She asked for my thoughts on the subject. My response: Jimmy has already been to hell, I doubt he booked a return trip.

There were two tragedies here. One was that Jimmy thought there was no way out. The other tragedy is that he was wrong about that.

Our paths have separated over the years, and we had settled into an annual Christmas phone call. I'm really going to miss that phone call this year.

FAQ

What's the worst drug out there?

The one you like the most.

My regular doctor said I have Bipolar, what should I do?

Get a second opinion. Medical doctors are great at tons of stuff, but diagnosing mental disorders is not one of their strong suits. My preference is using Psychiatric Nurse Practitioners for this task. As with therapists and rehabs, be sure to do your homework.

I'm dating a guy who uses pills every day. I love him and I have asked him to stop, but he won't. What should I do?

Find a new boyfriend. That will be good for both of you.

Does hypnosis work?

Sometimes.

Does acupuncture work?

Sometimes.

Does EMDR work?

Sometimes.

Does Alcoholics Anonymous work?

Sometimes.

Does anything work every time?

No.

Does anything never work?

Yes. Pretending it's not there never works.

Email the author at: larryvaughan@mac.com

Send complaints and criticisms to: complaints.com

Where I work: www.counselinglexingtonky.com

Made in the USA
Lexington, KY
02 November 2015